THE LITTLE BLACK BOOK OF COMMON CENTS

By: Te-erra Davis

The Little Black Book of Common Cents

ISBN 9781795852678

www.TheeFinancialCoach.com
Thee Financial Coach, LLC
610 Frederick Road
Catonsville, MD 21228
coach@theefinancialcoach.com

Copyright © 2019 by Te-erra Davis

All rights reserved. This book is protected by the copyright laws of the United States of America. No part of this book may be reproduced or transmitted in any form for commercial gain or profit without written permission from Thee Financial Coach, LLC.

Printed in USA

TABLE OF CONTENTS

HI! I'M TE-ERRA DAVIS... 9

INTRODUCTION 10

CHAPTER 1: CRAFTING AN EFFECTIVE FINANCIAL SPENDING PLAN 11
- My Intake 11
- Fixed Expenses 12
- Variable Expenses 12
- Non-Essential Expenses 13
- My Total Expenses 14
- Earn More Than You Spend 14

NOTES 15

CHAPTER 2: STAYING WITHIN YOUR FINANCIAL SPENDING PLAN 16
- The Envelope Method 16
- Tips to Reduce Your Expenses 17
- Energy Savings 18
- Food Savings 18

NOTES 20

CHAPTER 3: REDUCING EXPENSES WITHOUT AFFECTING YOUR LIFESTYLE .. 21
- Preferred Customer Programs 21
- Buy Used 22
- Online Shopping 22
- Ration Purchases Over Time 23

NOTES 25

CHAPTER 4: SAVING MONEY ON A DAY TO DAY BASIS 26
- How to Save 26

NOTES 29

CHAPTER 5: SHORT TERM SAVINGS 30
- Saving Strategies for Short Term Goals 30

NOTES 32

CHAPTER 6: LONG TERM SAVINGS 33
- The Power of Compound Interest 33

- Saving for College 34
- Student Loans and Government Aid 35
- Scholarships 35
- Saving for Retirement 36
- IRA's 36
- Traditional 37
- Roth IRA's 37
- 401K 37
- TFSA and RRSP in Canada 38
- Individual Savings Account in the United Kingdom 38

NOTES 39

CHAPTER 7: USING YOUR CREDIT CARDS WISELY 40
- Simple Credit Card Management Tips 40

NOTES 43

CHAPTER 8: GETTING OUT OF DEBT 44
- Credit Card Debt 44
- IRS 47
- Student Loans 47
- Car Loans and Other SHORT-TERM Bank Loans 48
- Mortgage Loans 48
- You Can Do It! 49

NOTES 50

CHAPTER 9: WAYS TO BRING IN EXTRA CASH 51
- Ways to Boost Your Income 51
- Use the internet to Your Advantage 52

NOTES 55

CHAPTER 10: SHOULD YOU REFINANCE YOUR MORTGAGE? 56
- What is Refinancing? 56
- What Does Equity Mean to You? 57
- Cashing Out Your Equity 57
- How to Get Started 59
- Modifying Your Current Mortgage Loan 59

NOTES 62

CHAPTER 11: CHECKING YOUR CREDIT REPORT REGULARLY 63

    WHAT'S IN YOUR CREDIT REPORT? 63
    HOW DO YOU GET YOUR CREDIT SCORE? 64
    ERRORS IN YOUR CREDIT REPORT 64

NOTES 66

CHAPTER 12: WHY A HIGH CREDIT SCORE IS IMPORTANT? 67

    MORTGAGE 67
    LOANS 67
    CREDIT CARDS 68
    JOBS 68
    CELL PHONES 69

NOTES 70

CHAPTER 13: HOW TO RAISE YOUR CREDIT SCORE 71

    ACTIONS THAT RAISE YOUR CREDIT SCORE 72

NOTES 74

CHAPTER 14: INTERNATIONAL CREDIT SYSTEMS 75

    CANADA 75
    UNITED KINGDOM 76
    AUSTRALIA 76
    INDIA 77

NOTES 78

CHAPTER 15: PROTECTING YOUR IDENTITY 79

    KEEPING YOUR IDENTITY SECURE 79

NOTES 81

SUMMARY 82

    FINANCIAL SPENDING PLAN 82
    SAVING MONEY 82
    THE POWER OF CHANGE 83
    TIME IS ON YOUR SIDE 83
    SEPARATION CAN RELIEVE ANXIETY 84
    CREDIT CARDS CAN BE YOUR BEST FRIEND... OR YOUR WORST ENEMY 84
    THE SCORE DOES MATTER 85
    DEBT MANAGEMENT 85
    MAKING EXTRA MONEY 86
    BOOSTING YOUR CREDIT 86
    AVOID YOUR OWN IDENTITY CRISIS 87
    SMALL TRANSACTIONS ADD UP 87

What You 'Need' is Often Just A 'Want' 87
   In Closing 88
SNEAK PEAK 89

Hi! I'm Te-erra Davis...

Respected by colleagues as an effective problem solver, Te-erra offers years of experience as a successful entrepreneur, leader, and financial professional. In her newly released series, "Money Mindset," Te-erra shares a unique and valuable perspective about the relationship individuals have with money and how their views effect their "Bottom Line." She shares practical recommendations of what everyone should do to change their relationship with money. Te-erra is also the author of, "The Little Black Book of Common Cents," "Love & Finance," "Keeping your marriage together," and "Resolve conflict in your marriage." All her novels are based off experiences she's gone through and how she overcame. Te-erra is actively engaged in personal growth and development while continuously sharing her progress year after year. In addition to her unwavering faith, Te-erra attributes much of her success to the training and development she received while attending Sojourner Douglass College.

As Brand Ambassador of Women, Wine & Business, Mindset Transformation, and Thee Financial Coach all under Thee Insurance Lady, LLC, Te-erra's personal mission is to educate and inspire each person one by one with literature, coaching, and seminars as she leads and impacts social change.

Introduction

In school, we spent *years* learning about science, language, math, and social studies from textbooks, but we spent *very little* time on *real* life skills like saving, making, and managing money. Somehow, we're supposed to just know how to manage our finances, as if it is instinctive to us! The truth is money management is *not* a skill we're born with – it is acquired. The good news is that you can *easily* learn the skill!

In the Little Black Book of Common Cents, we'll go over several key areas including but not limited to:
- Creating and staying with a budget
- Cutting expenses without sacrificing your lifestyle
- Saving money every day
- Getting out of debt
- Boosting your income
- Refinancing your mortgage
- How to boost your credit score
- Protecting your identity

Take time at the end of each chapter to reflect and implement the steps. After all, your financial success is up to you!

Chapter 1: Crafting an Effective Financial Spending Plan

The best way to acquire financial security is to have a sound plan. With a realistic plan, you can have more money to plan that dream vacation or buy that awesome big screen TV with the surround sound system. In order to indulge in these luxuries without *destroying* your bank account, you *need* a financial spending plan.

My Intake

The backbone of any plan is based on how much you make. Even if your income is lower than you'd like, you can still budget successfully, but it's important to know what you must work with in order to create a balanced plan.

When crafting your financial spending plan (FSP), it's critical that you use your *net income* (after tax dollars) as opposed to the gross (before tax dollars). Doing so will give you a more accurate representation about what you're working with while factoring in what the government takes as deductions. Funds being deducted from your paycheck is money that isn't yet available to spend. Then when you file your tax return, treat the refund like a bonus.

If you're a commissioned employee or business owner and your income is varied, using a close estimate should suffice in most situations. A realistic estimate can be gathered by totaling your income from the past 3-6 months, and then divide by the income you received in that time.

Fixed Expenses

There's no way around it; we all have bills to pay. Some bills vary from month to month, but there are others that are constant. Many loans are structured, so you pay the same amount every month. For example, your car or home payments are *fixed* expenses.

Some examples of common fixed expenses are:
- Mortgage or rent
- Car payments
- Car insurance
- Property taxes
- Home insurance
- Loans and lines of credit

Make a list of your fixed expenses and total the result.

Variable Expenses

This is where making a budget gets a little bit tricky. Not every bill is the same amount every month. You don't *always* spend the same amount at the grocery store or on gasoline. It's easy with the fixed expenses, but here there is room for error. Use an average amount of each variable expense for your budget.

The good thing about variable expenses is that you can change them. As you'll see, reducing these variable charges is a great way to keep more of your hard-earned cash.

Some examples of common variable expenses are:
- Car maintenance
- Gas

- Food
- Electricity
- Heating

List your variable expenses and total the result. A good strategy is to go through your recent credit and debit card purchases to see where your money is going.

Non-Essential Expenses

There will always be things that we *want*, but don't necessarily *need*. These types of purchases fit into the *non-essential expenses*. The difficulty here, is that we often confuse what we *want* with what we *need*. A good test of willpower before making any purchases is to ask yourself: "Is this a want or a need?" If you can't answer that question honestly, then give yourself 24 hours to think about it before deciding.

Some examples of non-essential expenses are:
- Excessive amounts of clothing and shoes
- DVDs, movies, books, magazines
- Video games
- Eating out
- Excessive gift purchases

Make a list of non-essential expenses and their total. Ask yourself: Do I *need* everything on this list? Is there anything I can cut out without losing the lifestyle I desire?

My Total Expenses

Write down all your fixed, variable, and non-essential expenses and add up the total. ***This total will be your base expenditure for the month.*** This is the bare minimum you'll need to make in order to have a balanced plan. If you make more, that's great. If you don't make more, then go back and look at your *variable* and *non-essential* expenses and find ways to lower these charges.

Earn More Than You Spend

The only way to create a workable FSP is to adhere to this one simple rule: ***EARN MORE THAN YOU SPEND.*** Obviously, your goal is to earn more than you spend, but if the numbers are close, that's okay; you can still work with that, but a wide gap would be ideal. Later, we'll discuss cutting costs and boosting income.

NOTES

Chapter 2: Staying Within Your Financial Spending Plan

Now that you've examined your income and expenses and created your financial spending plan, is it workable for you? ***The best plan is the one that works for you.*** As you use it, feel free to adjust the amounts in the expense categories according to your realistic needs.

For example, if you had designated $300 per month for gas, but the gas prices rise, you may need to go back and raise the amount in the plan. ***Keep your FSP up to date so you can continue to enjoy its benefits.*** Does your plan have workable amounts, but you find that you're still having difficulty staying within your budget? Try the *Envelope Method* to easily keep track of your spending in each category.

The Envelope Method

The Envelope Method requires you to move to a cash-only system. Although this may sound like a challenge, it's easier than you think! This technique is an easy 3-step process:

Divide and conquer. Each payday, ***cash your paycheck at your bank***, then divide the cash into different envelopes for each expense category. For example, label one envelope *Rent* or *Mortgage,* one envelope *Groceries,* one envelope *Car Payment,* and continue in that manner until you have an envelope for every expense. Include an envelope for daily spending money for things like lunch or parking. To determine how much to put into each envelope, look at your monthly budget and then divide the monthly expense by 2 if you get paid twice each month or 4 if you get paid every week. So, if you get paid every week and your grocery bill is $400/month, take $100 out of each paycheck and put it into the *Groceries* envelope.

Use cash for your expenses. Once your paycheck is divided up, it's very easy to keep track of your spending. That *Groceries* envelope, for example, is your grocery money for the week. ***Spend it wisely.*** Once you spend the money in that envelope, that's it for the week.

Effortlessly limit daily spending. Each day put the cash from your *Spending Money* envelope into your pocket or purse. That's your spending money for the day. ***When it's gone, stop spending!*** Making a separate envelope for each day's spending money helps you always stay within your budget without having to keep a mental figure of your balance in your mind.

Besides making it easy to limit your spending to the budgeted amount, the Envelope Method also gives you a better sense of your money. When you pay cash, you're more likely to see the real impact of your spending, even if it's small expenses. As you'll notice, small expenses *really* add up!

Tips to Reduce Your Expenses

If you find that you're spending more than you make, you have two options:
1. Make more money.
2. Reduce the amount that you spend.

There are many techniques you can implement to bring in more money. These methods are discussed in a later chapter dedicated to increasing your income.

It's usually more difficult to reduce your *fixed* expenses, though it's not impossible. For example, if you rent an apartment and your lease is about to expire, perhaps you can find an apartment that costs less. If your cable package features channels you don't use, inquire about changing to a less expensive plan. In the same way, you may be able to reduce your cell phone plan. *Most likely, you'll make cuts in the variable expenses.* Things like entertainment, food, gas, and even energy expenses can easily be reduced.

Energy Savings

With energy, it's simple to reduce your bill. Turn lights off when you leave the room and switch to more energy efficient bulbs. Unplug your electronic devices when they aren't being used, because they use energy even when they're turned off if they're still plugged in. If you have some money tucked away, newer models of appliances – like washers, dryers, and refrigerators – are also much more energy efficient and can pay for themselves in energy savings within a relatively short amount of time.

Food Savings

Buying groceries is a necessary expense, but one you have a lot of control over. A run to the grocery store can be devastating to your wallet if you let it, but it's also one of the best places to save money. Here are some excellent ways to reduce the amount of money you spend at the grocery store:

Sales. Most grocery stores usually do a good job of putting everyday items on sale. If you buy the product on a regular basis, you might as well take advantage of the discounted price and buy it when it's on sale. The savings on each item may not be much, but you'll find that a few cents deducted here and there add up quite quickly. Planning your weekly menu around what's on sale that week can turn into some significant savings.

Savings Card Programs. Plenty of grocery stores have implemented savings card programs, which give you a wider range of discounts to take advantage of. On rare occasions, they might even have a blanket discount, like 10% off the total bill, *Watch for these promotions.*

Coupons. *Your most potent weapon against the grocery bill are coupons.* You can find them in newspapers, flyers, and hundreds more online. These coupons can range from five cents to 100% off the cost of the item. You can't get better than free! While a coupon for a certain product may limit you to one product per coupon, you can often pick up several of that item by simply using a coupon with each item. It's easy to obtain multiple coupons.

Some stores even double the amount you see on the coupon, so you'll want to investigate which stores have such a program because it can add up to big savings very quickly. One thing you don't want to do is underestimate the power of the coupon! It's possible to buy two hundred dollars' worth of groceries, hand the cashier a stack of coupons, and only end up paying a tiny fraction of the price. Reducing your grocery bill by hundreds of dollars with coupons is surely a quick way to balance your budget while still eating like royalty!

Stockpiling. Buying in bulk has become a trend when it comes to grocery shopping. Stores like Sam's Club and Costco thrive on selling items in bulk at a low price. When used in moderation, buying in bulk can be a great way to save money. Be careful not to get carried away when shopping in stores that sell in bulk. Plan out what you may be able to use before the expiration date and shop accordingly. Keep in mind, also, the amount of storage space you have available in your home. One of the benefits of stockpiling is that you don't have to go to the grocery store as often. *Fewer trips to the grocery store save you time, gas, and grocery money.*

When you take advantage of these methods to save money on your regular expenses, it leaves room in your budget to increase your spending in other categories. In turn, staying within your budget becomes a whole lot easier!

NOTES

Chapter 3: Reducing Expenses Without Affecting Your Lifestyle

Entertainment, leisure activities, and lifestyle are often the first things to get cut when tightening the financial belt. It's unfortunate, but at the same time, this can save you quite a bit of money. Hobbies can be expensive, so it makes sense that this might be an effective way to reduce spending.

However, even though cutting yourself off entirely from your hobby (whether it be movies, books, comics, golf, or anything else) might be a good way to reduce spending, it may not be entirely necessary. In fact, leaving some money in the budget for relaxing activities is healthy and much needed! *There are ways you can reduce expenses without depriving yourself of the things you love.* If you keep your lid on straight, you can savor the joy of indulging yourself without the guilt of thinking about how it'll ruin your plan. There are quite a few ways to go about this.

Preferred Customer Programs

Like the grocery cards mentioned in Chapter 2, these loyalty cards reward you with gift certificates or cards for spending a certain amount of money. The standard rate is usually around $5 for every $100 spent, though it'll vary from store to store. Many times, the store will have some sort of event where you can earn double or triple points. For example, some bookstores offer a rewards program as well as a blanket discount for their preferred customers. This works in your favor on two fronts and if you can find a bookstore that has such a setup, *it's a great way to save money on things that you were going to buy anyway.*

Some loyalty programs will offer a discount of perhaps 10% off the price. Depending on what state you live in, this won't do much more than negate the sales tax, but money is money and it can add up to significant savings. So, look for preferred customer programs in stores where you spend your "fun" money. These programs can help you continue to enjoy your hobby while spending less.

Buy Used

A great way to save money on your hobby is to buy used items. Stores such as Wal-Mart or GameStop have sections reserved for used games or movies. Movie rental stores also sell used copies of movies and games. When compared to the price of a new item, there is usually a drastic difference. For the comic collector, many back issues can be found at a much lower price compared to the ticket price. There is also the option of trade paperbacks. Many comic readers have converted to that as it's often cheaper.

Book fanatics will also find that used bookstores are an advantage when it comes to saving money on their literary addiction. Paperback books are inexpensive, but a used one is even less. Spending two or three dollars as opposed to six or seven may not seem like much, but every little bit count.

Online Shopping

Another way to save money is to buy things online. With popular websites like Amazon or eBay, you can often find the item you're looking for at a price much lower than the one you'll see in any store. This also has the benefit of convenience as you don't have to go out to the store, saving you both time and money.

In addition to the low prices, Amazon will frequently offer items on sale. Most of the time, it's usually a couple of dollars (though discounts like that add up over time) but occasionally you can find expensive items for a drastically reduced price. Impulse shopping on the web can be a dangerous habit, but *with markdowns and a healthy dose of willpower to stop while you're ahead, you can save a bundle.*

Ration Purchases Over Time

There's nothing wrong with buying the things you want or indulging in a hobby. *You work hard for your money, so of course you'll want to treat yourself right.* It only becomes a budget issue when it causes you to spend more than your income. If you're a collector and you feel the urge to go out and expand your library of whatever your pleasure may be, a way to meet your wallet halfway is to buy these items at a reduced rate. So, if you're a movie fanatic, rather than going out and buying five or six new movies a week, reduce it to two or three every couple weeks, or rent the movies instead.

If you enjoy going out on the town for entertainment, rather than going out every weekend, cut it down to perhaps once per month, and enjoy the company of family and friends at home on the other weekends. It could be your house or theirs. Vary it for a change of pace! Maybe you have a gigantic Amazon wish list and you want to start putting a dent in that bad boy. Rather than whipping out your credit card and clicking compulsively until the card is maxed out, come up with a system where you pick items one by one.

Your system could be to allow one or two items each month, or you could decide to budget a specific amount, like $25 a month, for this one wish list. *This technique has the bonus of turning a variable expense into a constant one.* Even if you're a gadget junkie, you can still implement a similar system. Promise yourself that you won't go out and buy a high-ticket gizmo until the one you just bought is paid off. This will keep you from getting buried in debt. *It may take you longer to acquire the desired items, but you'll do it in a fiscally responsible way.*

Implementing this kind of purchasing program is also beneficial in the long term. For instance, when you get a promotion or raise, training yourself to ration out the indulgences will allow you to keep more of your money and give you financial breathing room later on down the line.

NOTES

Chapter 4: Saving Money on a Day to Day Basis

Everybody wants to save money, but few implement *lasting* solutions to help them save daily. There are all sorts of savings plans that will suit long term as well as short term goals. Even daily, you can find ways to tuck money away for a rainy day.

How to Save

Here are some easy strategies to help you get into a regular habit of saving money:

Create a separate spot for savings. Whether it's a sock drawer, an old wallet, or a separate bank account, one of the best ways to save money is to stash it somewhere and essentially forget about it. *Use the concept of "out of sight, out of mind" to put the money aside.* It can be the leftover money from your paycheck or even $10 a week, but if you make sure to put money aside consistently, you'll find that you can accrue a good chunk of change.

In this digital age we live in, you can set up systems like this automatically with your bank. With a few clicks of the mouse, you can have the bank transfer money from your checking to your savings account with no work needed on your part. Your bank can set up your transfers according to your preference, such as weekly, bi-weekly, or monthly.

Small deposits can add up quickly. Do you feel that saving money means you need to set aside huge chunks of dough in order to be worth the effort?

The truth is quite the opposite! Even if you can only put aside a couple of dollars here and there, that will add up later down the line. By using an interest-bearing savings account, you'll allow the interest to add to the savings. As the account grows, so too will the amount you receive in interest. This means that the longer you save, the easier it'll become. It may take a while, but once you get the ball rolling, ***the effect will snowball*** and allow the numbers to really climb.

Find bargains wherever possible. One of the best ways to save money is to keep your eyes open for money-saving opportunities and take advantage of them. For example, many of your day to day expenses can be reduced simply by changing your routine. ***If certain expenses are important to you then simply make your changes in other areas.***

Some financial experts talk about how, if you stop drinking Starbucks forever, you can become a millionaire. They use this logic to say that *any* spontaneous purchase is a devastating blow to your retirement. **Saving is important but viewing every purchase as a grievous offense is a faulty way of looking at it.** Keep your Starbucks, if you like, just find other ways to make up the difference.

Finding a more efficient solution can be a great way to keep more money in your pocket. If you enjoy having a soda while you're at work, rather than going to the vending machine and spending a dollar (or more) on a bottle, buy a 24 pack and bring it with you in a cooler. It's cheaper and it can save you a substantial amount every week.

You can use the same strategy for lunch. The best way to save money on lunch is to bring one from home. You'll find that the amount you spend on two or three restaurant meals could provide you with two or three *weeks* of meals from home. ***Save the eating out for when it's important to you.*** Even when money is tight, you can still enjoy seeing your savings grow when you combine automatic withdrawals with simple daily saving strategies.

NOTES

Chapter 5: Short Term Savings

Saving isn't only for the distant future. While that's all well and good, sometimes you'll want to save for a more immediate purpose. Maybe you want to take a family vacation or buy a new computer. Whatever the case may be, purchases like this require some *saving* ahead of time.

Saving Strategies for Short Term Goals

These techniques can help you effectively reach your intended goal:

Plan. The more prepared you are, the better. If you're planning a major event for your 20th anniversary, for example, you could start saving for it just after your 19th anniversary. If you're looking to upgrade your home theater system, look at the price and determine how long it would take you to reasonably acquire that amount of money.

All you need to do is find the price of the item, decide when you want to make the purchase, and then divide the price by the number of weeks until the purchase date. The answer tells you how much to put aside each week. ***Start planning for your special purchase well ahead of the event*** because the longer time you must save, the less money you'll need to save during each pay period.

The power of the change jar. Did you have a piggy bank (or some variation of it) when you were a child? Piggy banks instill the idea of saving money at a young age. Little did you know that the same principle could be applied later in life! ***Your extra change can be a very powerful savings tool.*** At the end of each day, simply put your left-over change into a container and leave it there.

It's rather brilliant in its simplicity. You usually round-up when you pay anyway, so as far as you're concerned, that money doesn't exist. As time goes on, the container will fill up and that jar of change will turn out to be a pretty hefty chunk of money. Roll up your coins and take them to the bank to trade them in. It may not be as convenient as those coin counting machines in the grocery store, but you'll save the 8% fee. Besides, you can make a game out of it with your kids. Or you can go to your nearest Credit Union to utilize their free coin counting machine.

Put off superfluous purchases. If you're saving up for a major purchase, a good way to speed up the process is to cut out any unnecessary purchases. You can always pick up the item after you get what you were saving for. Putting off unimportant purchases will make it easier for you to reach your goal.

The electronic change jar. A lot of banks have implemented automatic transfer programs that mirror the change jar. It started with Bank of America's "Keep the Change" program, where any debit purchase triggered a transfer of the difference up to the next dollar. For example, a $5.85 purchase would transfer $0.15 to your savings account. *Like the change jar, it's a great way to subtly put money aside.* One of the great perks is that some banks match a small percentage and add it as a deposit to your savings account at the end of the year. It's like getting free money just for saving your change!

Using these short-term saving tips will allow you to truly savor your end goal knowing that you paid for it in full. Imagine the pride you'll feel when you pay for your next vacation with the money you've already saved, instead of maxing out your credit cards. Then, it's even sweeter when you aren't overwhelmed with bills when you get home! Rather than spending the next year paying for last year's vacation (plus interest), you can get something else you want! And you can do it all by growing your savings in ways that don't make you deprive yourself.

NOTES

Chapter 6: Long Term Savings

Along with saving for your short-term goals and tucking some money aside for a rainy day, it's also important to implement long term savings. Long term savings are typically used for funding your retirement or your children's college expenses. Establishing a plan for long term savings can seem like a daunting task at first, but it's one you can accomplish if you put your mind to it. The great news is, with long term savings, *you can benefit drastically from the interest build-up.* Just as with short term saving, there are important things to consider in your long-term savings plans. For example, the longer you have for saving up, the less money you need to allocate each month toward your goal.

The Power of Compound Interest

Let's look at an example of the effect of interest over the long term. If you start a retirement plan when you're 25, and put in $100 per month for 40 years, here are your results at an 8% interest rate:

Total amount saved: $353,855.46

Total Principle: $48,000 ($100/month for 40 years)

Total Interest Earned: $305,855.46

Compare the two figures above. It shows you the power of compound interest. Over $305,000 of your savings is from interest alone! As your savings grow, you're getting paid interest on the interest you already received. So, it's in your best interest to *take advantage of all the interest you can* and start as early as possible on your long-term savings.

Saving for College

With the price of tuition skyrocketing at unimaginable rates, it's very important that you have a plan to prepare for these costs. Here are some strategies that can help you build a hefty college fund:

Start early. It's best to start a college fund in your child's first year, this will give you as much time as possible to save the necessary funds. You can set up an account in their name, set up a savings bond, or simply open an account in your name and allocate it as a college fund.

Assemble a team. Try to get other relatives involved. Most aunts, uncles, and grandparents are happy to contribute to a child's education. It doesn't need to be a drastic amount, but every little bit helps. Instill a good savings mentality in your child and *let them put their little piece into the pie.* Regular contributions from your child, even if it's only a dollar, teaches them the importance of saving, and *this value will benefit them for the rest of their life!* It also increases their college fund.

Seek security plus a higher interest rate. Browse around and find which bank has the highest interest rate. Online banks tend to have higher interest rates for savings accounts but do your research and see which one pays the best rates. As you deposit more money and the balance grows, so will the amount that the bank will pay you in interest. A difference of even 1% can have a big effect on your total savings.

Many investment products pay more interest than a savings account at your bank. Look into using mutual funds, exchange-traded funds, universal life insurance and other investments to increase your rate of return. However, *as the interest rate grows, so does the risk.* A college fund may not span enough years to tolerate much risk. So, keep safety in mind as you search for higher returns.

Student Loans and Government Aid

Even with savings in a college fund, there's a good chance that you or your child will need to take out some form of student loan to help pay the bill, especially if they attend an out-of-state college or pursue post-graduate degrees.

You can apply for a loan through your local bank, but the federal government also offers financial aid. Federal student loans generally charge lower interest, so it may save you some money.

In addition, unlike most loans, federal student loans don't activate immediately. Depending on the terms of the loan, *you can usually delay the start of payments until after your child graduates.* This allows the student to focus on his or her schoolwork. After that, there's often a "grace period" of a few months before the bills start rolling in. For more information on government-based student aid, you can go to:

http://studentaid.ed.gov/PORTALSWebApp/students/english/index.jsp

Scholarships

One of the best ways a student can save money on college is to get a scholarship. These can be offered on an academic or athletic basis. Some offer a completely paid-for education, while others cover only a portion of the fees. Of course, some is better than none. With the cost of education as high as it is, any assistance is beneficial. A major benefit of scholarships, of course, is that *you don't have to pay them back!*

When you do your research, you'll discover there are tons of scholarships available! If you'd like more information, visit your local bookstore or do some research on the internet. Also, once your child has decided on a college, **take advantage of the college's financial aid office.** This office gives you access to a multitude of scholarships available from the college's alumni association, as well as a host of other sources.

Saving for Retirement

Retirement is the big kahuna when it comes to savings goals and it's also the most important! The better you plan, the sooner you can reach your goals and retire free from financial stress.

While basic savings accounts may suit your needs for the most part, it's recommended that you investigate other investment services that can provide a better rate of return on your funds. There are 2 basic retirement accounts that are the preferred method for most working people, the 401(k) and the Individual Retirement Account (IRA), but please note there are various products designed to supplement your retirement. Take the time to research Supplemental Retirement Methods.

IRA's

IRA's are retirement accounts you can open with your bank. They allow you to create a portfolio of stocks, bonds, and mutual funds that will provide a much greater return than that of a simple savings account. There are two general types of IRA's, Traditional and Roth.

Traditional

The traditional IRA is the actual investment account. You can fund it with cash or cash equivalents, so while baseball cards and comic books can make great investments, you can't fund an IRA with one. One of the perks of the IRA is that the money you deposit isn't taxed. Basically, when you siphon off some money into that account it's considered "pre-tax" dollars. This allows you to legally keep some of your money away from Uncle Sam, at least for the moment.

When you hit retirement and start taking the money out, that's when they tax it and consider it your income. If you're going to deposit money into a traditional IRA, ensure that you don't need that money at all. *Taking money out of an IRA before you hit age 70 will incur penalties*, plus you'll have to pay income taxes on it as well.

Roth IRA's

Roth IRA's are different from the traditional, these aren't tax deductible. While the deposits are considered "after tax" dollars, it's much easier to get to your money if you need it with far fewer penalties involved. There's a deposit limit of $5,000 per year into your Roth IRA account ($6,000 if you're over age 50). If you have both a Roth and Traditional IRA, then that number applies to both accounts combined. The limit is still $5,000 or $6,000; it doesn't double just because you have two accounts.

401K

This is another option you have when it comes to retirement. Unlike IRA's, where you sign up through your bank, a 401K is done through your employer. 401K accounts have an annual deposit limit of $16,500.

Much like an IRA, any contribution will not be taxed until you withdraw from it. Earnings made from the 401K are also tax deferred until the money is withdrawn. Also like an IRA, taking money out of your 401K before you reach the minimum age (60 in this case) will result in hefty fees and penalties. One of the major perks of a 401K is that some employers match your deposits up to a certain percent. This will essentially put free money into your account and expand your nest egg quite significantly.

TFSA and RRSP in Canada

In Canada, you can get what's called a Tax-Free Savings Account (TFSA). You must be 18 or older in order to open a TFSA. You can withdraw money at any time without tax penalties. *While the deposits aren't tax deductible, money made from that account isn't taxed.* Canadians also have what is called a Registered Retirement Savings Plan (RRSP). This is much closer to America's Traditional IRA, only the deposit limit's much higher than that of America's. It also doubles as a 401K as employers can put money from your paycheck straight into the account.

Individual Savings Account in the United Kingdom

In the UK, you can get what is referred to as an Individual Savings Account. The ISA can be divided into two components: a cash component and then a stocks and shares component. It's possible to transfer funds from the cash to the stock's component, but not the other way around.

NOTES

Chapter 7: Using Your Credit Cards Wisely

Credit cards are convenient on so many levels. With credit cards, you don't have to carry large amounts of cash, you can pay quickly and easily, and you don't even have to pay immediately. While the benefits are numerous, credit cards also carry a serious responsibility.

It's very tempting to go on spending sprees or neglect to pay your bill on time, but *irresponsible use of a credit card can lead to severe financial repercussions,* including mounting debt, wasted dollars, harassment from bill collectors, lowering your credit score, and even bankruptcy! Fortunately, credit cards aren't a complicated concept. A good dose of common sense and responsibility will go a long way.

Simple Credit Card Management Tips

Follow these tips to manage your credit cards wisely:

Start with debit cards. Almost all checking accounts now come with a debit card. If you're considering getting a credit card, *it would be smart to start with a debit card as training.* A debit card operates in a similar capacity to a credit card: the merchant runs it through the scanner, and you sign the receipt. The only difference is that, where credit cards put off the payment, debit cards process the transaction immediately. This restricts your spending to *only* what you have in your bank account.

Only buy what you can afford. A good rule to follow when it comes to credit card use is to simply ask yourself if you have the money for your purchase. If you don't, then don't buy it. If you have a payday coming between the purchase and the arrival of the monthly credit card bill, you can usually flirt with the line, but when it comes to credit, it's usually better to err on the side of caution, especially if you're new to the world of credit cards.

Wait to buy high end items. There are rare occasions where it's not feasible to wait, like if you need immediate car repairs. However, most expensive items can wait until you save the funds to buy it.

If you do buy an expensive item, quit using the card until it's paid off in full. A major challenge you may face with credit cards is that you'll buy some large indulgence, and then you'll continue to use the card. Doing so makes the balance out of reach and nearly impossible to pay back at the high credit card interest rates. If you stop using the card until the item is paid off in full, the interest charges will be kept to a minimum and you won't find yourself drowning in debt.

Small purchases add up. Even more dangerous than the big purchases are the *little* ones. It seems absurd, but it's true. With a large purchase, you (ideally) go in knowing that this is a big deal and compensate accordingly. It's trickier with smaller, but regular purchases, like lunch or a tank of gas. We tend to dismiss small charges as insignificant: five bucks here and there. Before we realize it, we've racked up a large balance!

Keep track of your purchases. A good way to ensure your purchases don't spiral out of control is to keep track of all your purchases. A spreadsheet or even a small notebook should meet your needs quite well.

Pay off the card in full whenever possible. Ideally, when your credit card bill comes in, you'll be able to pay off the balance in full. If it's possible to do so, then do it. If you can't pay it off right away, then pay it as quickly as you can. Paying your credit card in full keeps you out of debt, saves you a ton of money on interest and fees, and helps raise your credit score.

Credit cards are convenient and can help you to maintain an excellent credit score, when used appropriately. They grant you power, and like any power, it requires an equal amount of responsibility.

NOTES

Chapter 8: Getting Out of Debt

While we all would love to pay off our credit cards in full every month, that doesn't always happen. Plus, modern life often *forces* us into debt. If you want to go to college, buy a car, or own a home, you'll most likely take out loans to pay for these things. Even if you do keep your credit card usage in check, it's difficult to remain *completely* debt-free. But fear not! While your mountain of debt may be intimidating, it's possible to get to the top and clear your financial name! First, let's tackle your credit card balances.

Credit Card Debt

Try these tactics to reduce and eliminate your credit card debt:

Pay off more than you use. The only way to gain ground on your credit card balance is to pay off more than you use. If you make the minimum payment of $20 and then spend $50, you're not going to be getting out of debt anytime soon. Also, be sure to consider the interest charge as well as other fees when calculating each month's total expenditure.

Pay off small balances first. If you have a card with a balance of only a couple of hundred dollars, paying that one off first will quickly eliminate one bill altogether, allowing you to reroute the money that would've gone towards paying that bill to one of the higher interest cards. This also eliminates the hassle of interest charges on that card. With no balance on the card, you'll be saving yourself in the long term as well.

Make high interest cards the priority. While the above rule is helpful in a handful of situations, you'll want to target the higher interest cards first and knock them out of the way.

Once a balance is paid off, use the money for that payment to pay off other balances. Knocking a credit card balance out is a major relief! It's one less payment you must worry about and one less monkey on your back. Use this success as momentum to take care of the other bills.

Utilize the following strategy to assist you in paying off your credit card debt. First, Pay off your first credit card with the smallest balance. Next month, Add the excess funds to your payment for your second lowest credit card. Pay this doubled amount on your second credit card every month until it's paid off. Once those two cards are paid off: Add the funds from credit cards 1 and 2 to pay on credit card #3. Pay this tripled amount on credit card #3 every month until it's paid off. Continue this strategy until you've eliminated your credit card debt.

This will greatly speed up the overall process of getting your cards paid off and wiping the slate clean. *What's amazing is that, once you've paid off your first card, you'll be able to use this strategy without paying more for your monthly bills than you were in the first place.* Yet, the momentum gets bigger and bigger for eliminating that debt, like a snowball rolling down a hill.

Avoid skipping payments. If you do miss a payment, they'll add the missed payment to the next month's bill *in addition to* the interest, late fees, and maybe even over-limit fees. This could even cause your annual interest rate to increase. Once this starts, it's difficult to get out of the pattern. The charges add up quick and your balance will skyrocket. Not only will this affect your balance, but the credit card company will also call you. Avoiding the call only makes things worse. You would think that they would get the point, but they don't. They call, and call, and call, and call. It's incredibly annoying and you're better off doing whatever you can to avoid missing the scheduled payment.

Debt consolidation can be your friend. Many times, it benefits you to consolidate several of your debts into just one balance from one creditor. *Not only can you take advantage of a better interest rate, but you also eliminate several of your monthly bills.* Often, the one payment on the consolidated balance is less than the total of your previous bills. If you can get a loan from the bank, it can help you out. Using that money to pay off your credit cards will reduce your overall interest charges. When going this route, avoid using your credit cards again after paying them off. That defeats the purpose entirely and will result in your debt becoming worse than it was before you started.

Many credit cards offer a lower interest rate for the first year on a new card, and they invite you to transfer your balances from your higher interest cards to your new one. On these offers, **be sure to read the fine print.** Many things, including one late payment, can void the initial offer and result in an increased interest rate even higher than you had on your old cards. Consolidating your debts can free up money that you can use to pay down your remaining balances. ***It's one more way you can get out of debt without using any more money than before you started.***

Use windfalls to pay down your credit card debt. If you come across some extra cash, use the money to pay off as many of those balances as you can. Your **windfall is multiplied** when you think of all the money in interest charges it will save you. Plus, the faster you become debt-free, the faster you can use your money for whatever you want rather than just sending it all to your creditors!

Eliminating your credit card debt can bring you immense relief and greatly enhance your financial future. But what about other types of debt? Luckily, there are some effective methods you can use to save money and pay off these debts in record time!

IRS

If you owe money to the IRS, make paying them off your highest priority! With their many fees and interest charges, a debt to the IRS costs you even more than credit cards, including possibly your home, business, and any money you have in your bank accounts. *Yes,* they can even go in and grab whatever is sitting in your bank account at any time! They can take your home or business and sell them to get the money you owe them. This is true even if your home is worth many times what you owe them.

Borrowing the money from a bank or charging what you owe to your credit cards is infinitely more beneficial than extending the time you take to pay whatever you owe to the IRS. Even refinancing your mortgage to get the cash needed to pay the IRS can be an option you may wish to consider. Whatever you do, don't mess with the IRS! Pay them off immediately with whatever resources you can gather.

Student Loans

In many cases, your student loans have a lower interest rate than your other debts, so they may not be as high in priority when it comes to paying off your debt. Also, you can often stretch out the payment period over many years, so the payments aren't a burden. However, these payments tend to add up because there can be multiple loans for every year of college. Plus, the total balance can be astronomical due to the high cost of attending college.

Check into consolidating these loans to eliminate multiple payments every month. Contact your lender(s) and see what programs they have for combining the loans. You may be able to continue receiving a low interest rate while only having to make one payment that's less than the total of your multiple payments. While consolidating can give you a handle on managing these loans, at some point, you'll want to finish paying these off also. Once you've eliminated your credit card debt, you may want to apply the extra funds towards this debt to get this monkey off your back as well.

Car Loans and Other SHORT-TERM Bank Loans

These types of loans usually carry lower interest rates than your credit cards. Depending on how long it takes you to pay off your credit cards, which are a higher priority, you may find these loans reach their term and disappear while you're paying off your other debt. In order to prevent car payments that never end, consider saving up the money in advance and paying cash for your next car. A used car, even if it only has 100 miles on it, costs thousands less than a new one and the original warranty is still in effect, just as if you had bought it new. Shop around for your best deal, both locally and on the internet.

Mortgage Loans

You can save tens of thousands of dollars in interest on your mortgage loan and pay it off 10 - 15 years sooner simply by restructuring your loan to an accelerated bi-weekly plan, instead of a monthly one. With a bi-weekly plan, you pay half of a regular loan payment every 2 weeks, instead of a whole loan payment once each month. The secret is, when you pay half a normal payment every two weeks, you end up making 26 payments in a year. This adds up to 13 regular monthly loan payments, instead of the 12 you would make on the monthly plan.

In order to set up your loan this way, you need to arrange it with your lender. It does no good whatsoever to just send in half of your regular loan payment. If you try this, the lender will either return it to you for sending in the wrong amount, or simply sit on it (with no benefit to you) until the other half of the payment comes in. This method is especially easy for you to implement if you get paid on a weekly or bi-weekly basis. So, make that call to your lender. The sooner you start, the more you save!

If you're getting a new mortgage loan or refinancing your mortgage, have them set up your loan this way in the first place. You'll be astounded at the difference. ***Alternatively, you can send in an extra monthly payment each year and have the lender apply it to the principal.*** The total amount you save may be less than with the bi-weekly structure, but it'll still reduce the mortgage by years – and thousands of dollars – by paying it off sooner. The trick in this method is maintaining the discipline to send in that extra monthly payment every year.

You Can Do It!

Paying off your debt can be difficult, but it's very possible when you use these techniques. Not only do these methods make it possible for you to be debt-free, but they can also save you many thousands of dollars in interest charges, making your debt-free celebration date arrive years sooner! When the going gets rough, just keep your eyes on your prize. ***Imagine what it'll be like to be debt-free.*** When you get your paychecks, all that money will be yours to spend as you please! No more mailboxes filled with bills for debt payments! No more harassing calls from creditors! Those debts aren't the boss of you, so take control of your debt today and enjoy the freedom that a debt-free life can bring.

NOTES

Chapter 9: Ways to Bring in Extra Cash

Working the standard 9-5 job may get the bills paid, but it rarely provides the financial cushion that we wish it did. Luckily, there are ways to boost your income.

Ways to Boost Your Income

Ask for a raise. Sometimes the simplest solution is the best one. If you have a good record and show that you're willing to work hard, most bosses will consider the idea of giving you a raise. Rather than make things more complicated than they need to be, why not start with your primary source of income and see if they can throw a few extra bucks your way?

Find a bank with better interest rates. This won't provide immediate relief, but it will add a little to your balance every month. If you're saving for the long haul, this can have quite an impact. Online banks like ING Direct tend to have higher interest rates than those of the "brick and mortar" companies.

If you decide to look for an online bank, be sure to make sure it's FDIC insured so you know your money is secure and the bank is reputable. *If you're happy with your bank, look at other types of accounts.* Money market accounts often offer higher interest rates than savings accounts while also allowing you to write checks. While there's a limit on the number of checks you can write, it's still convenient to have the best of both worlds in one account.

Get a second job. Although exhausting, getting an additional job may enable you to pull in enough extra income each month to make ends meet. It doesn't have to be a glamorous job, and even a part time gig can help you get back on your feet. Unless you really enjoy your second job, *this is a tip that's only to be used temporarily* for an extra income boost. Working yourself that much will burn you out and there are other things in life to enjoy besides making money.

Offer your services. A good way to pick up some extra income is to offer your services to others. Offer to babysit your neighbor's kids so they can go out, set up a lawn-mowing service in the summer, shovel snow in the winter, paint houses, and more. *Some of these services may help you pick up a few hundred dollars extra every weekend.*

Buy things at garage sales and sell them at flea markets. This can turn into a lucrative weekend pastime. You can find some real bargains at garage sales that provide great profits when you resell them.

Use the internet to Your Advantage

The dawn of the digital age has changed the way business works forever. Not only has it changed the way companies distribute goods, but *it has also given people the power to go into business for themselves* and advertise their services to a world-wide audience. If you're looking to make a little cash on the side, you have a variety of options at your disposal.

Sales. With sites like eBay, Amazon, Poshmark, Mercari, you can now put money in your pocket by selling things you no longer need. Have an old television, DVD, or Atari 2600 that you want to get rid of? Someone on the web will gladly buy it. *Sell all your unused stuff and clean out your clutter while making money.* If you liked the idea about picking up items at garage sales and reselling them for a profit, *you can also use eBay as another place to sell your garage sale purchases.*

Writing. The internet has given self-publishers an excellent venue to showcase their work. You can easily write "how-to" books (even short ones) and sell them through Amazon or Clickbank.com. Amazon has a program called Kindle Direct Publishing where you only need to upload the digital version of your book and they print and mail them out as they're ordered. This means no inventory since the books are printed on-demand.

You can also write articles and sell them. Some sites and business owners offer upfront payments for articles. AssociatedContent.com can get you started. You can also sell your writing services at Elance.com or WarriorForum.com. *If you're a stay at home parent, this is a perfect choice.* You get to work your own hours, write about topics that excite you, and make extra money.

Virtual Assistance. There are several small businesses who would love to have someone help them maintain and grow their business. There are several tasks that small business owners need help with, but they just don't have the time to do it themselves. That's created a huge opportunity for virtual assistants (VAs).

Some common tasks include answering customer support emails, updating and maintaining websites, managing social media accounts, bookkeeping, transcribing audio, creating presentations and videos, optimizing websites for the search engines, sales, and many other simple and advanced tasks.

Web Shows/Vlogging. The rise of internet videos has resulted in web shows. You could produce your own show on the internet. Some sites, like Blip.tv and YouTube for example, offer payment for your videos. The pay is based on how many times people view your video. Like any job, it has its fair share of stress, but it also allows for a lot of freedom and creativity. Likely, this venue would only produce some supplemental income rather than a primary income.

Blogging. Surprisingly, *blogging can become a lucrative business.* When you put up a blog on the internet about a popular topic, you can monetize it with paid advertising, sales of your own digital products, and commissions from affiliate products. Your set-up costs are minimal: A domain name ($10 at GoDaddy.com), hosting ($8 per month at HostGator.com) and blog software to run the blog (free at Wordpress.org). You can find people to set up your blog for you inexpensively and then get all kinds of good tips for bringing traffic to your blog and making a profit with it at WarriorForum.com.

Affiliate Marketing. If you haven't heard of Affiliate Marketing then here's a small definition, it is the process of earning a commission by promoting other people's products. All of us do this daily. We promote our barbers, nail techs, hairstylists, mechanics, etc.... Why not get compensation for your referrals. There are various Affiliate Marketing Programs, conduct some research and find the ones right for you.

As you can see, there are many opportunities to bring in extra income. *Use your creativity and talents to devise your own income stream.* Don't let the confines of your current job keep you from boosting your income elsewhere. *There's always something you can do for extra cash.* All it takes is a commitment to do it and the discipline to follow through with your plans.

NOTES

Chapter 10: Should You Refinance Your Mortgage?

Refinancing your mortgage can be a smart move if the benefits you'll receive outweigh the drawbacks. Obtaining a mortgage with a lower interest rate or lower monthly payments can be very attractive and can even save you *thousands* of dollars over the course of the loan. On the other hand, there are fees involved in the switch.

What is Refinancing?

To get a clear picture of the benefits available to you, it's helpful to know the process involved in refinancing your mortgage. Refinancing your mortgage consists of paying off the loan you currently have and taking out a new mortgage loan. Your current loan gets paid off in the refinance when you close on the new loan. **However, it's generally easier to obtain refinancing** than it is to acquire a mortgage loan in the first place. Depending on the amount of equity you have in your home, it's possible to make the switch without coming up with any cash up front other than incidental expenses, such as a new appraisal or title insurance. The closing costs, however, can all be rolled into the refinance.

Equity is the current value of the home minus what you still owe on it. Your equity increases each year as you make your mortgage payments and from the increase in the value of the home. For example, let's say you bought your home 5 years ago. The price of the home was $100,000, you put in a $20,000 deposit, and you took out an $80,000 loan. If your home's value increased by $10,000 each year, it's now worth $150,000, five years later. In the meantime, perhaps you've paid $3,000 on the principal of your home by making your mortgage payments. (In the first few years most of your loan payments go toward the interest, rather than the principal.) So, $150,000 minus $77,000 (what you still owe on the loan) = $73,000. You have $73,000 in equity on your home in this example. You started out with $20,000 in equity and, in 5 years, you've increased it to $73,000.

What Does Equity Mean to You?

Your equity is what gives you all kinds of choices in refinancing your home. The more equity you have as a percentage of the value of your home, the more advantages you have when you refinance. For one thing, for refinancing the home in the example above, you're now searching for a mortgage loan for only 52% of the total value of the home, rather than the 80% you were looking for in the first place. This opens a whole world of new lenders that would be willing to take on the risk of lending you the money.

Any time your equity is enough so that you're financing less than 70% of your home's value, it's much easier to find lenders that will compete for your business, even if your credit leaves a bit to be desired. In addition to making it easier to find a lender with more attractive terms than your original mortgage, *your equity can also make it possible for you to obtain a good chunk of cash,* which you can use to pay off your high-interest debts or make a major purchase.

Cashing Out Your Equity

When you receive cash along with your refinance, it's called "cashing out your equity." Keep in mind whatever equity you cash out in your refinancing process becomes part of the money you're borrowing with the new loan. For instance, in our example above, you owe $77,000 on your current loan. When you refinance, your new loan may be closer to $87,000 if they roll the closing costs into the new loan. You won't "feel" the costs of the closing, because you won't have to pay them in cash, but they exist and get rolled into the new loan.

If you wanted to cash out some of your equity, but you still wanted to keep under the recommended 70% re-financing threshold, you would first figure 70% of your home's value. At a $150,000 value, you could finance up to $105,000. So, let's say that the amount owing, plus the closing costs come to $87,000, ($77,000 is owed, plus $10,000 in closing costs), you could still cash out $18,000 and remain within your 70%. ($87,000 + $18,000 = $105,000)

If you have good credit, you could cash out even more of your equity and look for someone to finance 80% of the loan. This would give you another $15,000 in cash, but your new loan would be for $120,000 instead of the $77,000 you now have. Even with a lower interest rate, your mortgage payments would, likely, go up.

Refinancing your mortgage with an equity cash-out sometimes makes financial sense, even if you'd be starting out on a new mortgage loan for a higher amount than your current loan. You can pay off higher-interest debts or use the funds to make a cash purchase, saving yourself the interest you'd have to pay on taking out a loan for the purchase. If you've gotten advantageous terms on the new loan and the payment is easily within your budget, you may find that you're able to significantly raise your credit score, too. **Paying off your current debts and making your new mortgage payments on time will build some great credit!** Plus, you no longer must make multiple debt payments each month.

Even though starting over on your mortgage loan can seem disturbing, if you **set it up with the bi-weekly payment system,** where you pay half the mortgage payment amount every two weeks, instead of the full payment amount once each month, you can still pay off this new mortgage in record time! ***The question of whether you should refinance your home depends entirely on your financial situation.*** It could do you a lot of good or it might not be to your advantage. Your best option is to consult with a financial advisor who can review your own unique situation.

How to Get Started

If you're considering refinancing your home, a mortgage broker can save you some time and trouble in finding a lender. You can usually get a good recommendation on a mortgage broker from a reputable real estate agent. Your mortgage broker can work with you to find the most advantageous funding for your financial situation. Basically, you tell them what you're looking for in a refinance (lower interest rate, lower payments, or cash out) and they take care of the details.

Modifying Your Current Mortgage Loan

There are some situations in which refinancing your mortgage isn't an option. Unfortunately, with the downturn in the real estate market, many thousands of people have found themselves in an "upside down" situation with their mortgage. If the value of your home has *lowered* since you first purchased it, you could owe more on your mortgage than the house is now worth. If this has happened to you, and you wish to obtain more advantageous terms on your mortgage, you might want to explore modifying your current mortgage loan with your current lender.

The government has instituted some recent programs that give lenders an incentive to help you out. You may be able to lower the interest rate, your monthly payments, or even the principal on the loan by modifying it. However, most lenders have been slow to answer the call, and often end up foreclosing on the properties before they'll modify the loan. Most lenders won't even consider a loan modification unless you're at least 30 days overdue on your payment. Then they may tell you they'll consider it, taking up the time right up to the day they foreclose on it.

So, trying to get a loan modification can be challenging, but it can be done. If you have a regular income and your financial situation is such that you would have no trouble making your payments if they were only a bit lower, your lender may be willing to work with you. If this is your situation, contact your lender to apply for a loan modification. **Then keep in regular contact with them by phone and fax.**

- Contact the department heads for the various departments you work with as your application progresses.
- Send faxes to the specific departments requesting regular updates.
- Record your phone calls, if possible.
- Write down the name of anyone you speak with, the date, and a summary of each conversation.

The internet has many resources that can provide you with valuable knowledge for working with your lender. Just do a Google search for "Mortgage Loan Modification" and do your research for the full details on the loan modification process and how you can work with your lender. With good communication and knowledge of how to make the process go smoothly, your loan modification can be a success. If you're not upside down on your mortgage loan and you've built up some equity in your house, *it's usually in your best interest to examine refinancing your mortgage* rather than trying to modify your loan. Generally, refinancing is less stressful and more successful than a loan modification.

NOTES

Chapter 11: Checking Your Credit Report Regularly

Currently, it's incredibly important that you keep up to date on your credit report. Your credit score plays a vital role in many essential areas of your life, including loans, renting a home or apartment, mortgages, and even your job.

Your credit score is determined by information gathered by three separate credit bureaus. These are Experian, Equifax, and TransUnion. *As a consumer, you're entitled to one free credit report from each bureau every year.* In addition, you may obtain a free credit report when you've been turned down for credit within the last 60 days. These three credit bureaus developed a central service to make it easy for you to obtain your free credit reports. Their website is: https://www.annualcreditreport.com. Through this service, you can request your credit reports be delivered to you online, by phone, or by mail.

What's in Your Credit Report?

Your credit report contains:
- Your name and any other names you've used
- Current and previous addresses
- Your record of payments on your credit cards and loans, including your mortgage
- Public records such as bankruptcies, judgments, foreclosures, and car repossessions
- Your credit limits on each of your credit cards or other lines of credit
- How long you've had each type of credit
- The balance due on each credit source
- If you've defaulted on any of your financial contracts

> Anything that was turned over to a collection agency, like outstanding bills

Most of the information stays on your credit report for three years. However, serious events like bankruptcies and judgments can stay on your credit report for seven or twelve years, depending on the type of bankruptcy or if it was a judgment.

How Do You Get Your Credit Score?

Although you have access to a free credit *report* each year, currently the credit bureaus do not include your credit *score* in your report. They charge a small amount to provide you this information. When you request your report, you'll have an opportunity to purchase your score also, if you so desire. Some credit monitoring services also provide your credit scores as part of their service. These companies charge a monthly fee for you to have constant access to your credit reports and scores and notify you of new activity on your credit reports. Such a service can alert you to any suspicious activity, like identity theft, which is an important concern these days. You may want to consider such a service if it would make you feel more secure or if you're actively involved in working with the bureaus to get things corrected and raise your credit score. With the credit monitoring service, you'll be able to see your changes are being taken care of.

Errors in Your Credit Report

Likely, there are errors in your credit reports. In fact, this is more common than you may think. Therefore, it's important to check your reports regularly, at least once each year. You may find addresses where you never lived, other people's credit cards, and even their bankruptcies and judgments. This false information can take a serious toll on your credit score and make it very difficult for you to get a loan, car, cell phone, or even a new job.

Unfortunately, *creditors tend to believe everything in your credit report whether it's true or not,* so it's best to get the errors corrected *before* you need to get a loan or go job hunting. If you find errors in your credit report, contact the bureau that's reporting the error and request that they correct it. For the most part, they'll contact the creditor and correct the information. In the case of certain disputes with creditors, you can also have it listed on your report that the case is disputed. You may also need to contact the creditor directly and have them correct the error.

Here are the sites where you can report errors on your credit reports:
For Equifax reports: http://www.investigate.equifax.com
For Experian reports: http://www.experian.com
For TransUnion reports: http://www.transunion.com

Checking your credit report regularly and getting any errors corrected in a timely manner will ensure that the information they're reporting about you is accurate. It also helps you to be proactive in working to raise your credit score, which will bring you an excess of benefits. We're going to discuss this in the next chapter.

NOTES

Chapter 12: Why a High Credit Score is IMPORTANT?

Your credit score can have a major impact on your life. Of course, this impact could be positive or negative, depending on your credit score. The higher your score, the more benefits it brings you.

Mortgage

One of the most notable impacts that your credit score will have is determining what kind of mortgage you can qualify for and even if you can get one at all.

If you have a poor credit score, you may get less than desirable terms or be denied for a mortgage altogether. Or they may tell you that they can get you financing if you come up with 50% of the cost of the house in cash.

A higher credit score will enable you to qualify for lower interest rates and a lower down payment. A lower interest rate not only saves you money on your monthly payment, but over the course of the loan, it can mean a difference of many thousands of dollars to you. You may be thinking you'll just rent. While it's true that renting an apartment doesn't require a loan, they may run a credit check to make sure you're able to pay the rent. A poor credit score may even keep you from getting an apartment, leaving you with little housing options.

Loans

Mortgages are essentially huge loans, so if your credit score impacts your mortgage, it stands to reason that it would also affect other loans such as student loans, car loans, or smaller bank loans. *Not having access to these sources of money because of a poor credit score can make your life much more difficult than it needs to be.*

The higher your credit score, the better chance you have of securing a reasonable loan when you need one. In addition, *many of the great deals you see advertised only apply to those with good credit.* For example, you may see an ad for a great deal on a car with no down payment. When you get to the car dealership to take advantage of their offer, you find out that it's only available to those with a high credit score. Whenever you see "W.A.C." in small letters at the bottom of an ad, it means "with approved credit." The lower your credit score, the more you'll have to pay for many items that you need or desire.

Credit Cards

While you'll continue to get "pre-approved" letters from credit card companies, the chances they'll grant you credit drastically reduces if you have poor credit. *Your credit score will also determine your interest rate and credit limit.* So essentially, if you want to go out and buy high end stuff with your credit card, you'll need good credit in order to get a suitable limit. They don't just hand out limitless cards' willy nilly!

Jobs

If you have poor credit, it may be more difficult to get a job if the employer does a credit check. The reasoning behind this is people with good credit are less stressed and more in control of their life. They may also be more able to focus on their job. A person with poor credit might also be more likely to steal from the company to pay their bills, so why take the risk? As ridiculous as this may sound, it's the reality of today's job market. It does, however, provide motivation to keep your credit in good standing. With a down economy and companies laying off employees left and right, you never know when you may be looking for a job. Plus, moving up to a better job is easier with a high credit score.

Cell Phones

Even cell phone companies inspect your credit history when you make a purchase. Like every other organization, they want to know that you can pay your bills on time. If you're a fan of texting, tweeting, web surfing, or even old-fashioned phone conversations, it's in your best interest to keep your credit score on the high end. Your credit score seeps into so many areas of your life that it only makes sense to keep it as high as possible. A higher credit score saves you all kinds of money, brings you opportunities not available to those with low credit scores, and makes your life a lot easier.

NOTES

Chapter 13: How to Raise Your Credit Score

There are so many variables that go into your credit score, everything you do in your financial life can affect it one way or another. With this in mind, let's look at how some simple actions can raise or lower your score. Here are some things that will damage your credit score:

Applying for a credit card. The simple act of applying for a credit card can hurt your credit if you apply too frequently. If you apply for several cards at once, it'll do serious damage to your score.

Spacing your applications out over time does less damage at once, but it lengthens the time it takes you to build up your total credit limit. Having high limits with low usage helps your score, but brand-new cards can also lower it. *Even though new cards can lower the score a bit, it still helps to build up your limits over a reasonable amount of time.* The credit score boost you'll receive once these cards show a wise record of usage is more than the temporary cut from when each card is new.

Using your credit card. Another factor in your credit score is your credit to limit ratio. This is essentially the fraction of how much credit you've used compared to how much you have. So, the more you use your card, the closer you get to your limit and the lower the score.

However, you must use the card occasionally. You see, if you just let that credit card sit in your wallet untouched, the company that issued the card may cancel it due to lack of use. *For a higher score, use your cards every so of-*

ten, but keep your usage to less than 25% of the total amount of credit available to you.

Canceling your credit card. That's right. Basically, once you have a credit card, you need to keep it. A lot of people make the mistake of thinking that closing unnecessary credit accounts will help their score. This is incorrect. In fact, it will lower your credit score as it lowers your total credit limit and affects your "credit age," doing damage on two fronts.

It seems that regardless of which way you turn, you end up lowering your credit score, which just begs the question, "How am I supposed to get a high credit score when everything I do damages it?" Fortunately, there are also specific actions you can take that will raise your score.

Actions That Raise Your Credit Score

The best way to raise your credit score is to pay off your current balances. This will widen the gap between your credit balance and your credit limit. While having cards clear of debt is nice, you'll want to use your cards enough to keep them active. ***Each month, charge something to your card and then pay it off before the payment due date.*** This will build excellent credit without you having to pay any interest charges. As time goes on, the fact that you kept those accounts open for as long as you did will lean in your favor when calculating your credit score.

While keeping your balance all on one card may be convenient for you, it's better to **spread the debt around to all your cards.** While the total will still be the same, this will reduce the balance on each card and that will work in your favor. This also helps form a sort of "revolving door" of debt. If you set up the cards so that some are due early in the month and others are due around the middle, you can set up a system where there is always a balance on at least one card at any given moment. *This will show creditors that you're willing to use your cards without going overboard, thus boosting your credit score.*

Lastly, *check your credit report at least once each year* and make any necessary corrections. This will keep you informed of what's going into your credit reports and alert you to any suspicious activity. Another strategy is to get your free report from a different bureau every 4 months. Alternating your reports in this way spaces it out to where you only request one from each bureau once each year, so they're all free, but you keep up with more current information.

NOTES

Chapter 14: International Credit Systems

While this book on money management goes into detail regarding the system of credit in the USA, other countries operate within their own unique credit system. *However, the principles of managing your credit, such as paying your debts promptly, still apply regardless of which country you may call home.*

In any country, lenders are about to whom they extend credit. Naturally, they want to ensure that any money they lend will be paid back in due time. It may be their business to lend money, but their profits are made when they receive it back with all due interest and fees. With this being said, let's look at a few of the varieties of credit systems you may encounter.

Canada

Canada has a similar credit system to that in the USA, but there are some key differences. They have 2 major credit bureaus:

- Equifax Canada: http://www.equifax.ca
- TransUnion Canada: http://www.transunion.ca/sites/ca/home_en.page

Canadians can request a free credit report as frequently as they like if the request is made in writing and the report is delivered by mail. Requesting a report has no impact on their credit score, although it is noted in reports. They also can submit a 100-word statement to be included in their credit reports.

Another difference is the length of time transactions and events remain on their credit reports. Most items stay on the reports for 6 years. In some areas of

Canada, bankruptcies remain on the reports for 7 years unless you file 2 or more times. In this case, they both will show up on the credit report for 14 years. The Financial Consumer Agency of Canada publishes a helpful booklet to help you navigate successfully through Canada's credit system and offers many helpful links for managing your debt in Canada. Their website is at: http://www.fcac.gc.ca/.

United Kingdom

The UK also has 3 major credit bureaus:

- Equifax: http://www.equifax.co.uk
- Experian: http://www.experian.co.uk
- Call credit: http://www.callcredit.co.uk

You can get a copy of your credit report from each of the credit bureaus each year for a very small fee. In the UK, there are additional things that affect your credit score that might surprise you, for example, voting. Registering to vote can boost your score, while not registering to vote can lower it.

Australia

Australia also has many complicated formulas for calculating your credit score. To access your credit reports in Australia, go to the websites of their 3 major credit bureaus:

- Veda Advantage: http://www.mycreditfile.com.au
- Dun and Bradstreet: http://www.dnb.com.au
- Tasmanian Collection: http://www.tascol.com.au

India

The Credit Information Bureau (India) Limited, or CIBIL, is the go-to place to find out about your credit in India. This bureau is a private partnership between banks, credit information service providers, credit card companies, and more. You can also purchase a copy of your credit report. Their website is at: http://www.cibil.com.

As you can see, even though they may have a slightly different credit reporting system, each country still has a way to determine your creditworthiness. No matter where you are, it's still important to manage your debt wisely for best results.

NOTES

Chapter 15: Protecting Your Identity

Identity theft has become a greater challenge than ever with the advances in technology. Unfortunately, there are several ways that your identity can be stolen and abused by the selfish and greedy. While the methods to steal your identity are many, there are also some solid ways to prevent others from obtaining your vital information.

Keeping Your Identity Secure

Follow these strategies to help keep your identity safe:

Shred all documents. Do you find yourself discarding your credit card bills or pre-approval letters without giving a second thought? While the credit card companies do what they can to ensure your privacy, it's still possible for someone to take your identity with the information available on each bill. ***Shred all mail that contains personal information.*** Be thorough when shredding your documents. Simply tearing them in half won't do. An inexpensive electronic shredder will save you time and help protect your personal data.

Sprinkle and spread remains throughout the garbage. Much is made about how these identity thieves are willing to rummage through your garbage. When throwing away old statements, be sure to spread all the pieces of paper around to ensure minimal chance of reassembly. Place a few pieces of paper at the bottom, add a layer or two of trash, and then put in more. You can even "sprinkle" the bills all over the bag and ***get them all mixed up with the rest of the garbage.*** Also, add as much miscellaneous garbage to the bag as possible. The more they must rummage through, the more secure your identity is.

Avoid suspicious emails. Email phishing is one of the most common ways for thieves to get your information. Most of the time, you can recognize it as the spam that it is. However, identity thieves have gotten better at hiding behind official labels. Only open emails from people and businesses that you know and trust. Avoid clicking on any links in your emails, particularly for banking sites or online stores you've shopped at. It's best to input known addresses into your browser and access websites manually rather than click a link in an email.

Keep your adware/anti-virus software up to date. One way that hackers can get your information is through spyware and viruses. Keep your software active and up to date to avoid this data theft. ***Run a virus scan on your computer at least once or twice each week.*** If you spend a lot of time on the internet and browse many sites, it's a good idea to run a scan every day. Regularly clear out all temporary files and your history and run disk cleanups to get rid of any junk that has accumulated on your hard drive.

Avoid putting personal information, like credit card or banking data, in emails that you send. Emails are a non-secure environment that can be easily hacked. If you need to send private information, put it into a locked PDF file and attach it to your email. Then give your reader the code to unlock it by phone, fax, or in person when you see them. Or just call it in, instead of emailing it.

Ensure you're on a secure site when giving personal information. A secure website will start with *"https"* instead of "http" and your lock icon at the bottom of your computer will appear.

NOTES

Summary

We've discussed several personal finance topics, so as we come to the end, it's a good time to look back over all that was discussed and summarize the most important points of managing your money effectively.

Financial Spending Plan

While crafting a plan sounds like a frightening task, really, it's quite simple. All that's required is that you **keep track of how much money you have, earn, and spend.** Most plans divide expenses into two primary categories, *fixed* and *variable*. But we add a third called: *non-essential* expenses.

The fixed expenses remain the same from month to month, such as rent or a loan payment. The variable expenses, like electricity and food, change from month to month. While the numbers change, you can still create a solid figure by averaging out the total purchases for each month. The non-essential expenses, like excessive amounts of clothing or entertainment expenses, are often thought to be *needs*, when they're really *wants* that are unnecessary to lead a happy and healthy lifestyle. If your expenses are *greater* than your income, you'll need to find a way to **earn more than you spend,** whether it's through making more money, spending less, or a combination of the two.

Saving Money

One of the best ways to maximize your income is to minimize your spending. Depending on where you shop, you have a variety of options when it comes to saving. For grocery shopping, keep an eye out for coupons. You can often find coupons for items you buy frequently. While one coupon may not do much, it can be a huge relief to the grocery bill when used in mass. The effect is expanded when some stores double the value of coupons to give you greater discounts.

For entertainment, search for used items as opposed to new ones. Many stores, including Amazon.com and eBay.com, offer the same products in good condition for a greatly reduced price. If you're a big collector of books, movies, or video games, this is a great way to cut that expense, while satisfying your urge to buy things. Find out if your favorite stores offer a preferred customer program. This can give you access to better sales, as well as gift certificates, that save you money on the things you were going to buy anyway.

The Power of Change

You may dismiss change as useless, but *it's a powerful savings tool.* Find a jar or container and empty your change into it each day. You'll be surprised at how quickly it adds up. When cashing in your change, take them into the credit union to save the counting fee from those machines at the supermarket. The saving power of change is so apparent that banks and credit unions have tweaked the concept for their debit cards. Rather than put the change in a jar, they'll transfer the change to your savings account. Ask your financial institution if they offer this type of savings program. Depending on the institution, they may also match a certain percentage, giving you an extra deposit every year. It rarely amounts to much, but everything helps. Why not boost your savings by using the card to buy things you were going to anyway?

Time is on Your Side

When it comes to long term saving (for things such as college or retirement), it's beneficial to use time to your advantage. In other words, *the earlier you start the better.* Not only does this give you a bigger window to earn the money you need, but the interest you earn will accumulate and increase as time goes on. This will make your money work for you to a much greater degree. Most people in their 20's doesn't even consider their retirement. In fact, it would be a safe bet to say that retirement is one of the *last* things on their mind. However, that is the best time to start saving up so you can let your nest egg grow to its full potential. Even a few years will greatly affect the amount of money you would've earned in interest.

Separation Can Relieve Anxiety

Most saving methods involve putting the money aside so you can't spend it. Indeed, "out of sight, out of mind" can be used to your advantage. Whether it's a separate bank account, a different wallet, or even hiding the money in your sock drawer, ***putting the money in a place where you won't think about it is a great way to get into the saving habit.*** Storing your money in a sock drawer or under your mattress is fine, but a bank account of some kind is a much better option. In addition to your deposits, you can make extra money in interest, which adds up over time.

Credit Cards can be Your Best Friend... or Your Worst Enemy

Credit cards are very convenient and grant you a lot of freedom, but with that freedom comes responsibility. If they're not handled wisely, credit cards can become a great liability. Prepare yourself for credit cards by starting off with a debit card. You get the same sense of freedom while knowing the outcomes of running the card through the reader. This will give you the discipline needed to properly handle a credit card.

The Score Does Matter

Your credit score can have wide reaching ramifications on your everyday life. Things that can be affected by a low credit score are:

- Ability to get a mortgage
- Ability to rent an apartment
- Your interest rate on loans and credit cards
- Your credit limits
- Cell phone service
- Finding a job
- Acquiring insurance

Suffice it to say, a low credit score can be devastating to several facets of life. Keeping your credit in good condition will benefit you in all of these areas. Good credit can also save you a lot of money with lower rates on loans and can enable you to live in a better house or apartment.

Debt Management

The best way to manage your debt is to start before you become overwhelmed. ***Pay off your credit cards in full every month*** and avoid just making the minimum payment. Sooner or later, you'll find yourself with debt, whether it's through student loans, car loans, or a mortgage. There's no sense in adding to that with high credit card balances. When it comes to paying off your credit cards, the best way to get out of debt is to pay more than you use in any given month.

Target your highest interest cards first in order to get out of debt faster. In some cases, paying off the smallest balance is a great way to kick start the process and to eliminate a whole payment as well as a set of interest charges. When you've paid off a credit card or loan, use the money that would've been used to pay that bill and put it towards another one. This will start a snowball effect that'll get you out of debt faster and save you money on interest charges. Paying off debt will save you money by eliminating the interest charges, that way you can start saving for your short-and-long-term goals.

Making Extra Money

The internet has provided a convenient way to make money on the side. Whether you're a writer or aspiring film maker, there are websites and small business owners offering to pay for your services. It usually isn't enough to make a living, but it can bring in a healthy chunk of change and make for a second source of income. Selling items at flea markets or on websites, like Amazon or eBay, can bring in some extra income on a one-time or regular basis. Offering your services can easily infuse another $1,000+ into your income each month.

Boosting Your Credit

Your credit score can be lowered by:
- Applying for too many credit cards
- Using your credit card and missing payments
- Canceling your credit card
- Not using your card and letting it sit idle

Looking at the list, it may seem like everything you do damages your credit score! All you really need to remember is to keep your balances low and to pay off as much of the bill as possible. Rather than keeping all the purchases on one card, try to spread it through all of your cards to keep the individual credit-to-limit ratios low. **Missing payments is a bad idea.** It allows the debt to accumulate much faster and it also results in a never-ending flood of phone calls. Missing even one payment can result in a much higher minimum payment and higher interest charges.

Avoid Your Own Identity Crisis

Identity theft is becoming a more serious threat as technology advances. People will go to great lengths to get your money and it's important that you take precautions. **Shred all credit card bills or pre-approval notices before throwing them out.** Make sure that they're ripped and torn beyond recognition and scatter them throughout the everyday garbage to ensure that no one tries to put the pieces back together. When working online, ensure that your anti-spyware and anti-virus software is up to date. Avoid fishy emails and websites. *When shopping online, be sure the site you use is safe and reliable.*

Small Transactions Add Up

When using your credit card, be cautious of small purchases. It's common to dismiss these charges as nothing while you continue to use the card repeatedly. With big purchases, you have a sense of awareness that you don't have when buying a tank of gas or a sandwich for lunch. The good news is this works both ways. By setting aside a small amount of money every week into a savings account, it'll continue to grow and grow over time! While being able to save large sums of money would be preferable for anyone, often, it's not realistic. If you save what you can, you'll be on your way to a financially comfortable life.

What You 'Need' is Often Just A 'Want'

It's tough when you're in a store and see something you really want. You may convince yourself that you can "afford" it or that the money doesn't matter.
As an isolated incident, this mindset is usually harmless, but it becomes a problem when this forms a pattern of behavior. ***Spending more than you pull***

in will put you on the fast track to a debt and stress crisis. If you can put off the urge to buy stuff, you can discipline yourself to only buy things when you can afford them. Smart financial management boils down to making more than you spend. If you can follow that one rule, you're ahead of the game!

In Closing

Money management is an important part of life. Saying that money makes the world go around is an amusing overstatement, but there's some truth to it! In order to get the things that you want in life, you need money. *Knowing how to handle your finances will make it much easier, while also leading to a more comfortable lifestyle.* Effectively managing your money is all about gaining the necessary skills, implementing the strategies, and exercising self-control. It may seem formidable at first, but once you get into the habit of saving, making, and managing your money, *you'll enjoy the freedom from fear, stress, and worry!*

SNEAK PEAK

Money Mindset

5 Book Series

ORDER YOURS TODAY!

GO TO www.TheeFinancialCoach.com

Changing Your Financial Outlook with the Proper Money Mindset

If you look at the profiles of wealthy people, you will find they have a different mindset than others. They know the value of money, and they know the fundamental factors of how to make their money grow. If you are not yet wealthy and feel you are struggling, take some tips from these wealthy people.

An age-old idiom of money is to use compound interest in your favor. Benjamin Franklin was a big proponent of this principle. He was quite wealthy for his time, so it is likely he knew what he was talking about. But it makes sense. If your money grows on its own, and the money that you earn ends up growing as well, it's only a matter of time when this amounts to a decent sum of money. And if you keep adding to the balance, that money will also grow along with it.

The situation is a bit more complicated today with government taxing the growth of money. But you can invest in an IRA or 401K and have that tax deferred until some future period. Speaking of taxes, make sure you work with a qualified accountant and a financial planner to ensure you are paying the least amount of taxes possible. Wealthy people do this.

Another principle wealthy people adhere to is creating multiple income streams. The more income streams you have working for you, the quicker you will become wealthy. When you have multiple income streams, pump up the ones that are working well and dump the ones that aren't.

After you are financially well off, make sure you never touch the principal. Set up your principal so that it earns the most it can earn and live only within the means of the earnings on that money. If possible, add to the principal with as much of the earnings as you can afford, so the principal grows. Just never tap into it. If you find any shortfalls, consider taking on some temporary work. Once the principal is gone, it's gone for good.

The final tip is to stay out of debt as much as possible. The debt will drain your savings and your portfolio. There can be smart uses of debt as long as the result of using that debt brings in more money than the debt itself. But most debt should be avoided to keep your financial outlook stable.

Is Your Money Mindset Setting You Up for Failure?

People want to make money. You see the lavish lifestyles of celebrities and other famous people and wish you could have the same lifestyle yourself. But, is your drive for money blinding you to what is truly important in your life?

It is often said that if you do something you love, the money will follow. There seems to be something to this because you will approach whatever you love with passion. You'll get better at it to the point where you are better than everyone else, or at least that is what you strive.

On the other hand, if making money is your driving force, how will you accomplish that? You will simply chase the dollar from one job to the next or from one opportunity to the next. You will get seduced by false offers of riches. Over time, you will look back and see that not much has been accomplished.

You may be successful in the short term of getting that extra dollar from a new job or squeezing a quick buck from your business. But you will constantly be in search for more money. You could even put yourself into a position where you can't handle the new job because you lack the necessary experience. In other words, you didn't give your previous level enough time to develop a foundation. You jumped ahead, and now you are unclear what to do. It's a concept known as the Peter Principle, named after the person who came up with the idea, Peter Drucker.

Money isn't as important as many try to make it out to be. For instance, what good is having a high-paying job when you must work 80-90 hours a week? What kind of life is that? Many people who do this, look back at their lives and wonder why they did it. While they may have a lot of money when they get older, they likely don't have anyone to share it with. Another possibility is the heavy workload to obtain that wealth gets them to an early grave. The money they earned is useless to them if that happens.

If you are happy with what you are doing, money becomes a secondary priority. People do need money to live, and you shouldn't settle to work for less than you are worth. But, when you can balance a decent amount of money with doing something that you enjoy, it will bring a whole bunch of satisfaction into your life.

Set Your Money Mindset to Passive Income

It's 6 A.M. on a Monday. The alarm is buzzing loud and piercing. You were having a great dream, and it's being interrupted by that darn alarm. You put it on snooze and go back to sleep for five minutes. After which, you go through the same routine: snooze and sleep. Finally, you check the time and decide you have no wiggle room. It's time to get up. You need to get to work with some aspect of being on time.

This routine happens five days a week. You are exchanging your time for dollars. Putting vacations aside, if you don't work, you don't get paid. If you work part time, you probably don't even get a vacation. If so, you are truly trading hours for dollars. Could there be another way?

You need to build up passive income streams. This gives you the ability to earn money without putting in any hours. Of course, they do need to be set up, to begin with, and that could take a fair amount of time. But, once they are set, they bring you consistent income on a frequent basis. It's almost like having your own printing press at your disposal.

When these passive income streams are ready to go, you could take a vacation, and you are still earning money. You could even be earning money while you sleep. The more of these streams you set up, the more money you make without having to trade your precious hours. Also, as these incomes grow on a monthly basis, you could replace your regular income. There's nothing bad about that!

How do you go about creating income streams? One example of a passive income stream is investing in dividend stocks. You will need an initial outlay for this, once you have this, you will collect cash on a quarterly and for some, a monthly basis. If you reinvest your dividends, you can build your portfolio to the point where it's earning some decent cash for you.

Another way to go about creating a steady income stream is to create a membership website. People sign up and agree to pay a monthly fee to you. Their credit cards get billed each month automatically. You have to make sure you keep a high level of quality on your membership. Otherwise, you are going to have a high unsubscribe rate, and this defeats the purpose of a membership.

Te-erra "Thee Financial Coach" Davis

Wants to Hear from You!

Tell Te-erra how
"The Little Black Book of Common Cents"
has impacted your life.

Email Te-erra at Coach@TheeFinancialCoach.com

Send Written Correspondence to:
Te-erra "Thee Financial Coach" Davis
640 Frederick Road
Catonsville, MD 21228

Review the Little Black Book of Common Cents at:
AMZN.TO/CCENTS
To Receive your **FREE** Little Black Book Financial Spending Plan Workbook

Get more insight, resources, and upcoming event info at:
www.TheeFinancialCoach.com